To Blossom And Bloom

Lauren J Barton

ISBN: 978-1-914288-74-6

Instagram: @ljbpoetry

All illustrations and front cover by Lauren J Barton

for one whole year she fell asleep
sucked into the void
into the deep.

If we want to serve the world
we must first serve Ourselves.

Contents.

DARK COCOON.

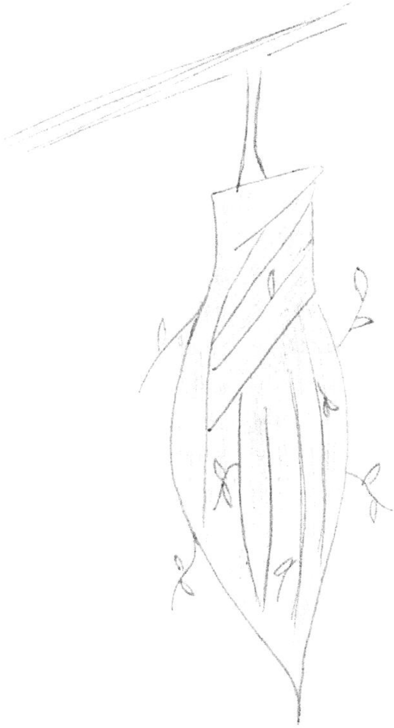

heavy eyes hide no lies
truths surfaces to the skin
washed up wounds from the battering of tides

naked and bare for everyone to stare
and gasp at the pain that's inside
my bruises lay sore
every mark keeps the score
of the damage irreversibly done

for my eyes cannot lie
sacred portals to my soul
and i must confess
right now

soul is numb

you told me i was beautiful today
proof that i can distort my outer reality
proof that external appearances and internal feelings often
don't match up

incredible how deceiving your shell can be

emotions are powerful

listen carefully

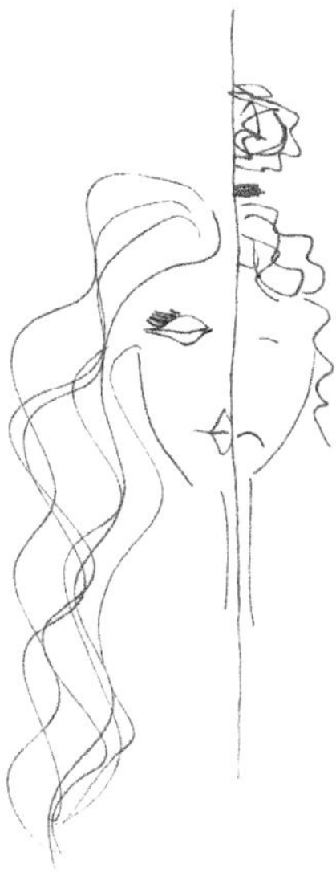

such a shame to waste the days
when the world feels grey
and your mind's in a maze

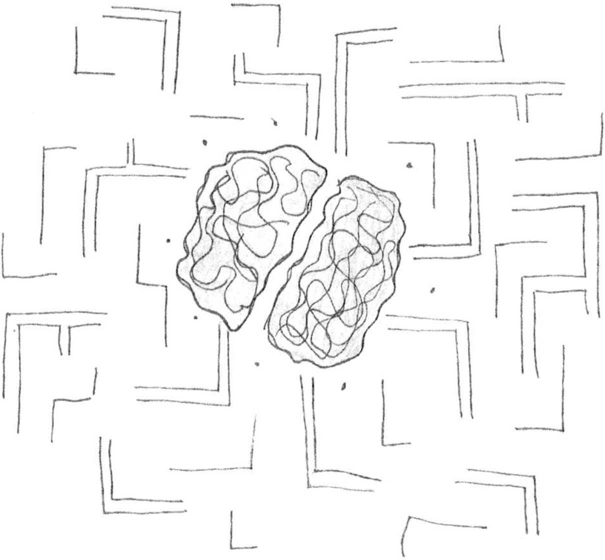

Anxiety 1.

you burn in me
like the wildest bushfire i ever did see
i must not add fuel to your flames
so hard to control
when you enter my soul
and urgently course through my veins

the difference between a wildfire and the fire in me
a wildfire has no ceiling
it eventually disperses in the air
but my body
she acts as your roof
you rattle my bones
n' bubble beneath the surface of my skin
with no means of escape
nowhere to go
so you stay
and paralyse my truth

perhaps though
if i give life to you
if i breathe you out
if i move you through me
consciously
and ask you nicely to leave
would you?

for there is only so much fire i can take…

i have listened to what you have to say
and appreciate your concern
i honour your purpose to keep me safe
from the wild
- still so much to learn

but it's time for you to go
as through me you will not grow

so simmer down
burn out
fire brigade
fire go

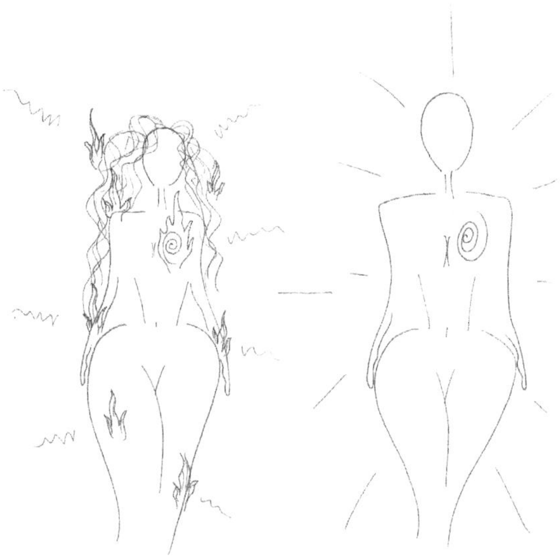

real tired tonight
i'm finding writing you a struggle
my focus wears thin
can't seem to reign it in
and my thoughts float all in a muddle

Mish mash

Stop

Body sighs

Sleep.

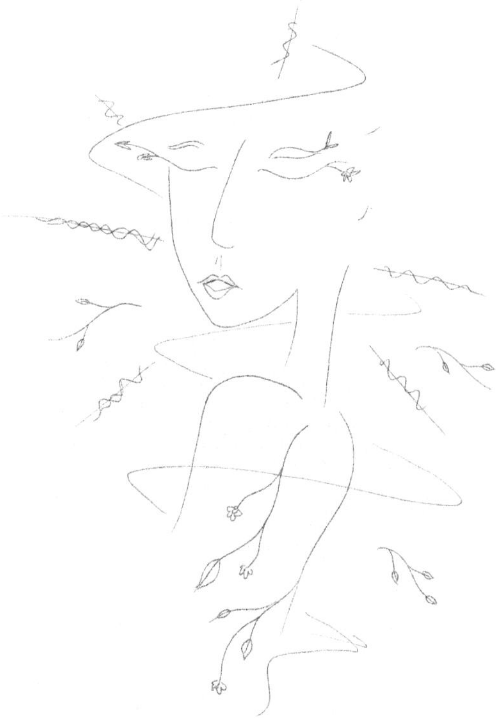

Anxiety 11.

i turned my anxiety into matter today
i pretended my hair was you
i wrestled with your stubborn knots
clawing my way through

your embellished ways
they had me dazed
as you entwined yourself in my hands
it felt powerful making you tangible
and destructing your devilish plans

you were powerless under my constraint
as i weaved my way out your maze
fire and anger my guiding force
i purged out
my red hot rage

peace at last…

you vanished for a while
well
metaphorically so

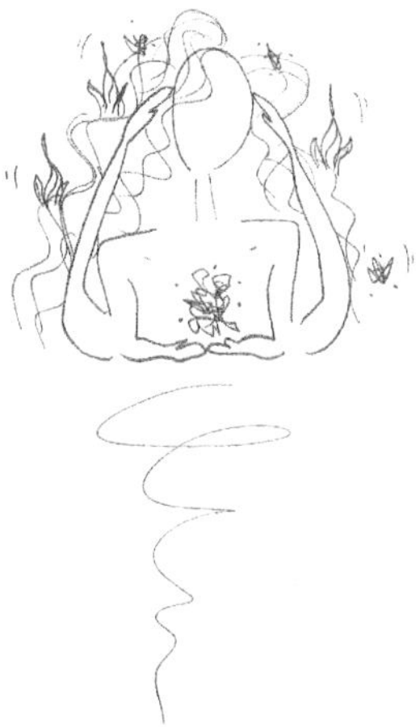

as your presence will come again
and dwell
all to well
this i dread
but know

my soul is exhausted
trying to save my heart from my head

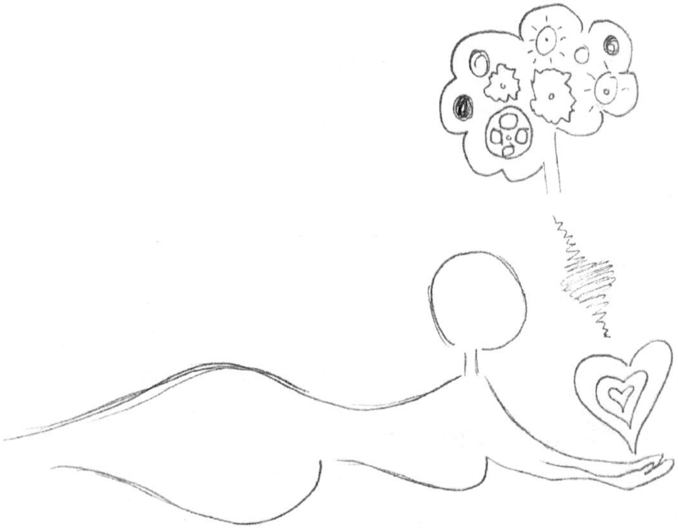

Anxiety 111.

i really thought that you would pass
that peace would come and surrender at last

but a home you have made
in my mind you have stayed

so a spell of good riddance

i now cast

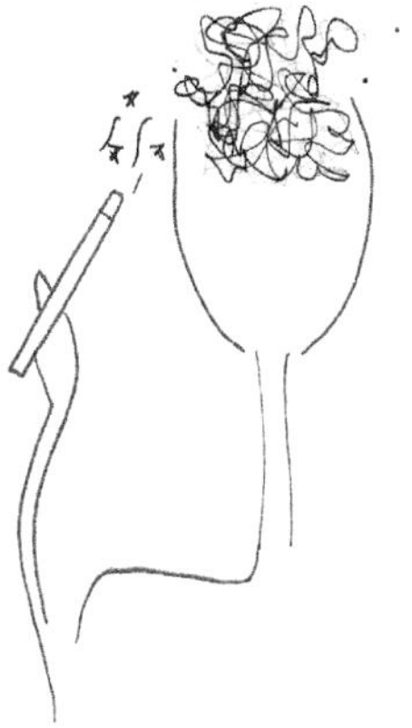

i'm tired of my mind today
please stop
calm down
give me rest
i beg
i pray

Anxiety IV

what is it you want from me this time?
you bled me dry
had my faith on the line

i'm exhausted from all your games
what are your intentions?
only one thing left to mention
you carry so
much ugly
shame

please leave me
alone.

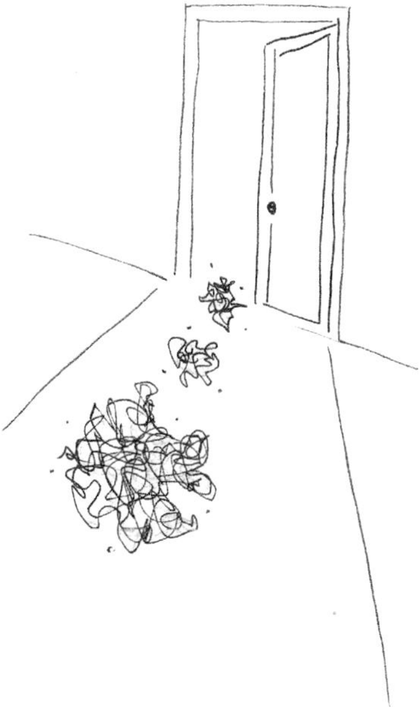

i wish it was easier to let people see
the vast spectrum of worlds living deep inside of me

- wildly misunderstood.

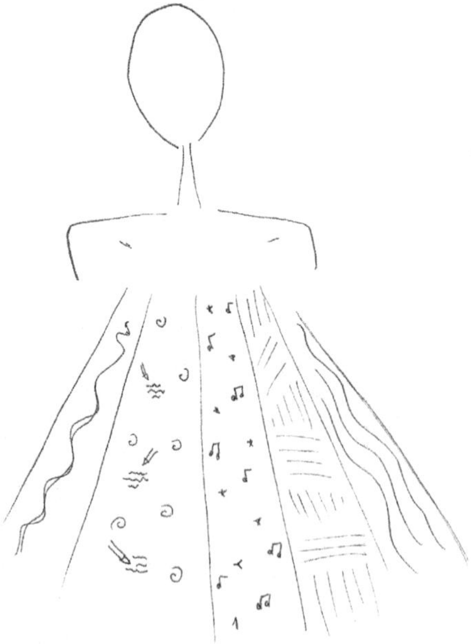

Pressure fear

fear that i'll let the pressure get to me
that i'll withdraw how i do
and not fight my way through
my resistance

my demons

it won before
but second chances no more

i wish my heart could talk
it beats so fast in my chest at times
begging for attention
i hope to make sense of you some day
i hope to make you proud
i listen as best i can
but forgive me
sometimes my mind
can scream so loud

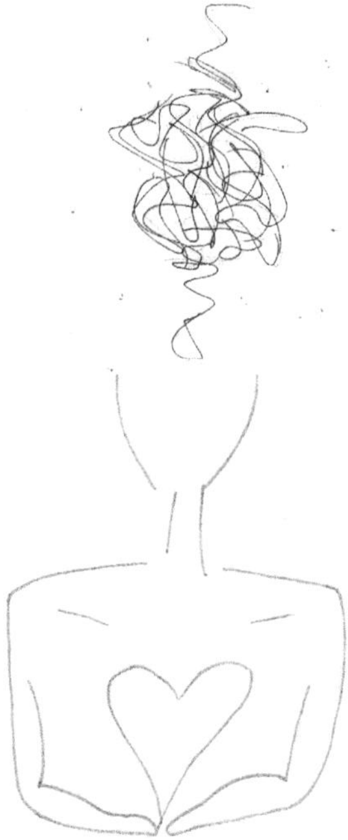

tryna rewire my brain
tryna save myself from going insane

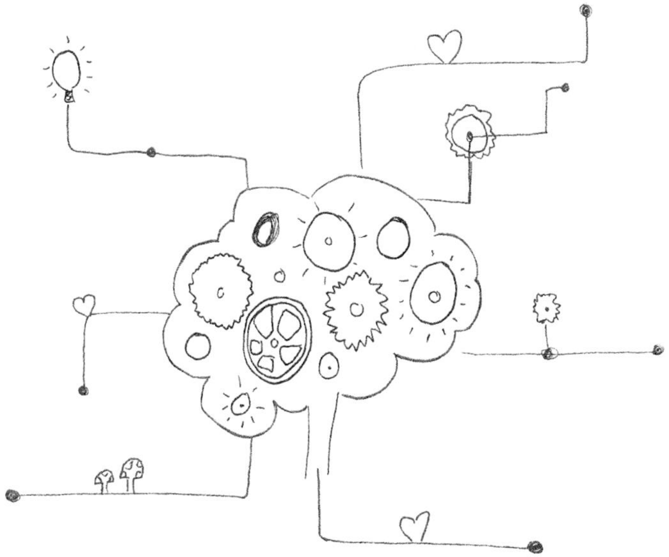

how is it possible to feel so of this world
yet so detached from it at the same time?

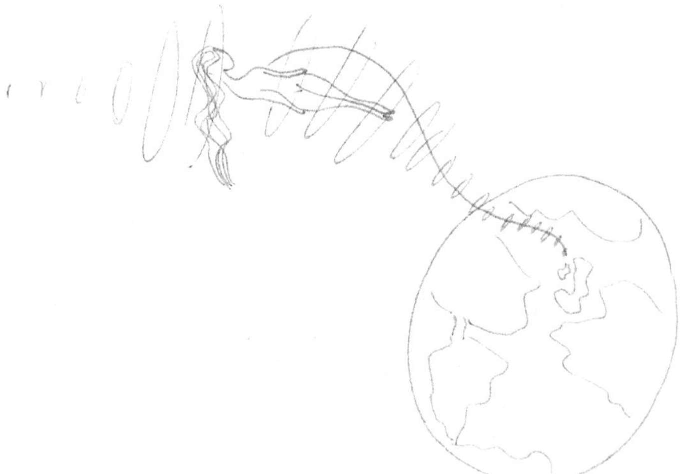

i'm afraid one day i'll have to put you to rest
not now
not for a while
not till i've got you off my chest

you cause storms of deep swells to arise within me
the kind of storms that take strength not to let others see

you bring me right to the depths of my core
you cause floodgates to open
and leave me feeling unsure of myself
i'm concerned for my own mental health
for my mind she is racing
heart too

but to honour your voice
is to accept
God's choice
so pen to paper
and write
i must do

- Relentless Muse

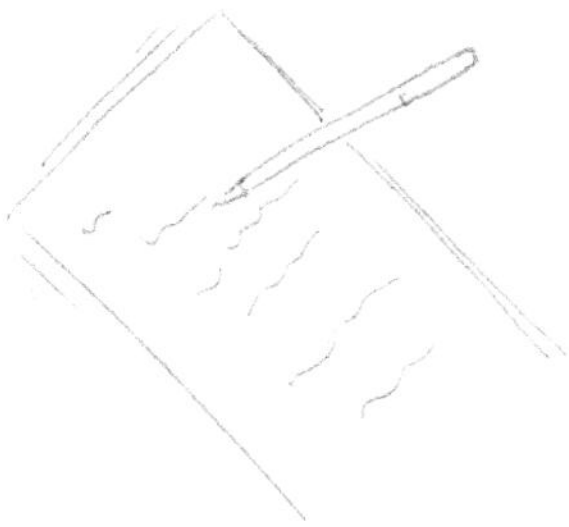

i thrive in solitude
however will it be
with another
with a lover

sharing space
we shall see

another night in my mask
to hide social anxiety
in a sea of lonely people…

lock the door
hide the key

a room full of people

no thanks
not for me.

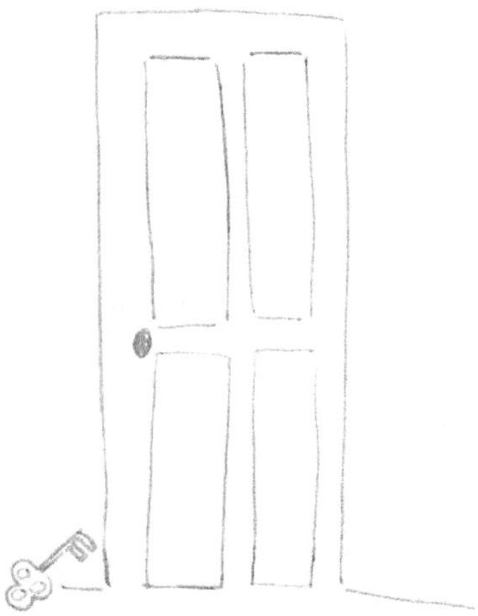

there's a tug at my heart
other worlds pull me apart

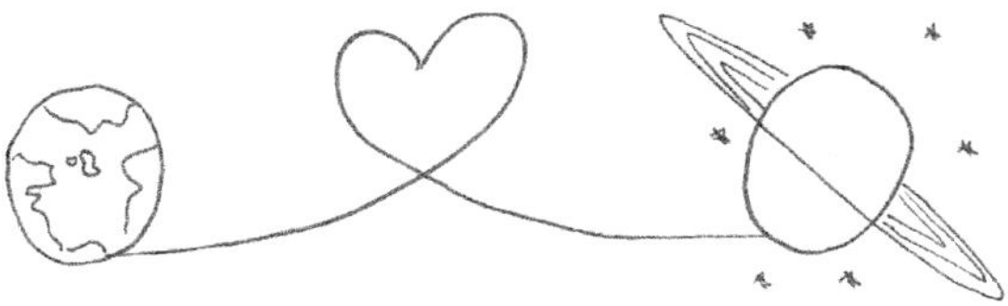

is life just gunna pass me by
am i always gunna be
more alive in the scenes of my dreams
stuck in matrix reality schemes?

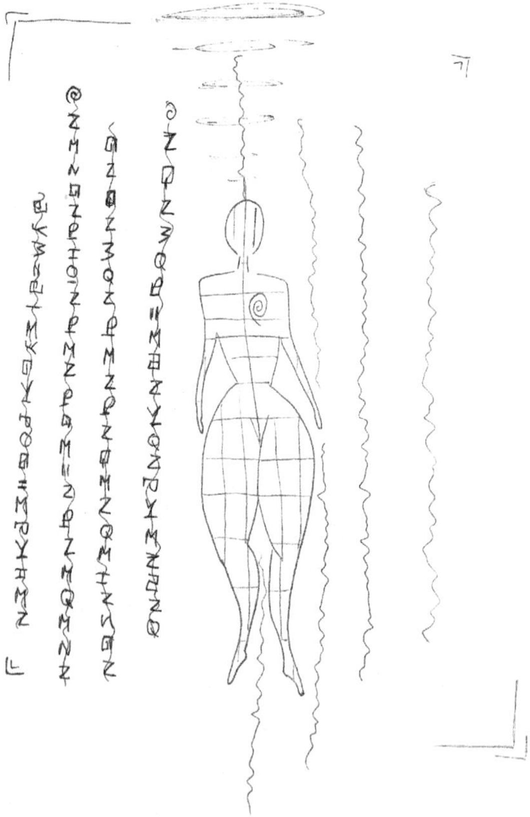

People

where are all my people
when will i laugh again with people

how do i engage and interact
are my social skills still intact?

when will one smile again with her people

worlds from minds we have made
so long up here we have stayed
for far too long we have obeyed
I miss
people
people
people

I long to sing again with my

beautiful
beautiful
people.

Covid 19. 20 - 21

i thought the problem was solved
but it only re-evolved

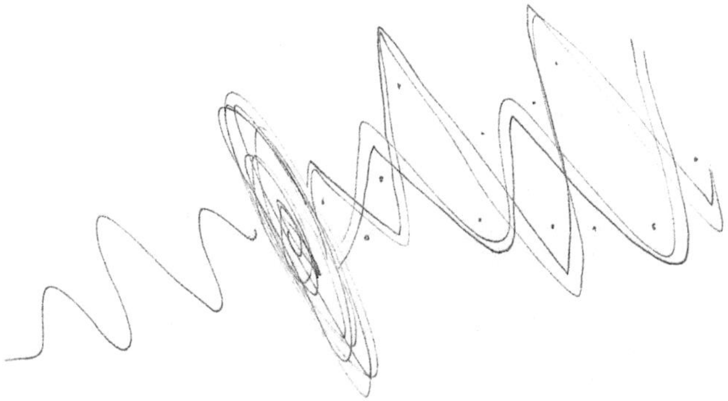

how can my mind want something so different from my
heart
why does it always feel like they are living worlds apart?

when will they learn to coexist

one day

i hope

i pray

sometimes the hurt leaks out of me
i can hardly see the wood through the trees
all the ways it destroys and suffocates my soul
as if possessing my heart
is hurts one and only goal
i didn't mean for my blood to spill
i was blinded by rage
my brain didn't know what else to do
it's time i turned a new page

i hope you understand
as i know you've felt it too
i realise now
in time

sit with pain

heal

it's the only way through

the only thing dutiful
left here to do

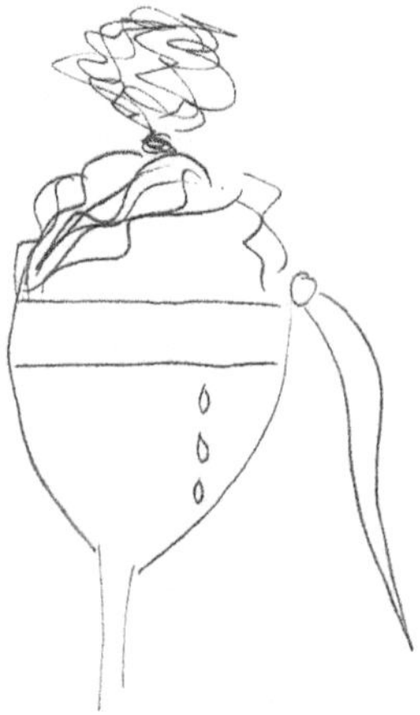

blessed to have known the devil.

RUDE AWAKENING.

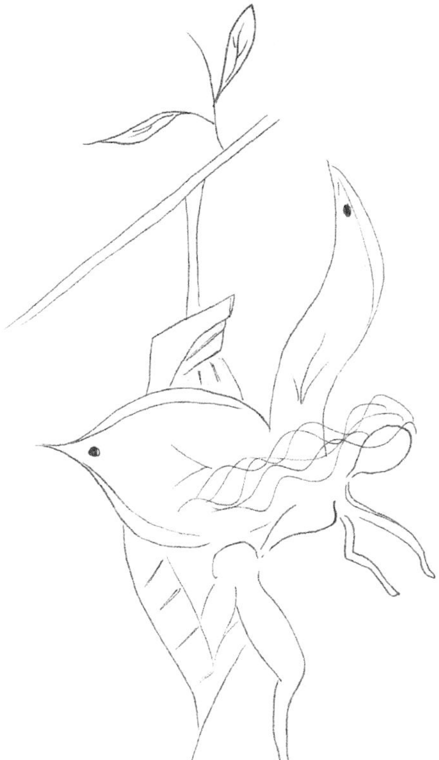

it would be nice to only know love…

but i guess that's not the purpose of living.

Hi I'm Grief

we've met before
you seem to dislike me
that's ok
its normal
i get it

well hey again!
ummm yea so this time…
your sister passed away
as you know
so i've been sent to help you through this stage of your life
it's a tricky one but if you let me help you
i can help ease your pain

i'll be honest with you
i'm not going away
as much as you would like that
even if you push me
i've been instructed to stay
until you finally give in
and surrender to being friends with me :)
peer pressure at its finest

as you can see my favourite colour is grey
what's yours?
grey too!
what a coincidence!

oh black
black at the moment
i see…

well you know black is a shade of grey
and at the other end of the spectrum
it's a pretty lovely bright white
it's one heck of a ride to get there
but such a beautiful wholesome sight

take my hand
trust me
i've got you

just keep holding on

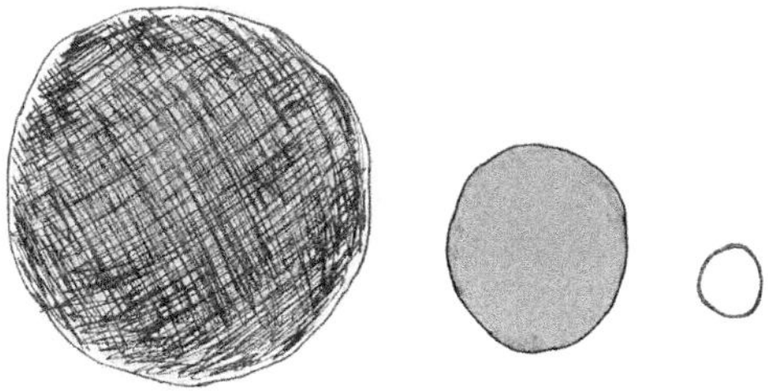

My Biggest Fear

IN-Q's prompt

~ strange
this has been on my mind so much lately
consuming me at every waking moment
meeting me in sleep too ~

i can't seem to get no rest bite
from the overwhelming sense of urgency
to hurry up on my life
it leaves me stranded
helpless
engulfed in fight or flight
see time has become my biggest fear
the fragility of life makes precious time so dear
to our hearts
i fear time slipping away
time melts and dissolves with each passing day

a sacred chart of the stars was designed to map time
each dot uniquely positioned over us as they align
i wonder did the ancients act in haste?
was there ever the need to quicken their pace?
something tells me that this was not so
they woke with the sun
and slept when day was done
never rushing
moving steadily in flow
never having a million places to go
allowing optimal space to be seen and heard
to heal
fully blossom
and grow

they trusted in the stars
in divine timing
why were we never taught this at school?...
see the only concept of time i know
is that faint relentless tick
every second a new flick
made by man and his eager ego

another mastermind invention
to add some more tension
to our shoulders
was that part of the plan?
please mr clock on the wall
i beg you to fall
cause now i'm forever
you least favourite fan

where did this fear come from, you ask?
when the clock has its uses and perks
i agree to some extent
but when riddled with grief
i find time isn't really what works

at first
it can smirk at your pace of getting things done
whilst you trudge through the mud of your pain
time evaporates and spoils
all the life that it boils
and the panic makes you feel less than sane…

i never much questioned this concept before
until time shook my core and death stood at my door

see
my sister she passed
a revolution she cast
to help us realise
that time is on loan

so now i wake with sun
i sleep when day is done
for time
i invent on my own
precious time is so delicately on loan

so strip away the ticking clock
there's ancient wisdom to unlock
unveil the illusion
evolve back to what was known
please rejoice into all you have grown
as you cherish the fruits you have sown

for time my sweet dear
is the only one thing
that none of us
will ever truly own.

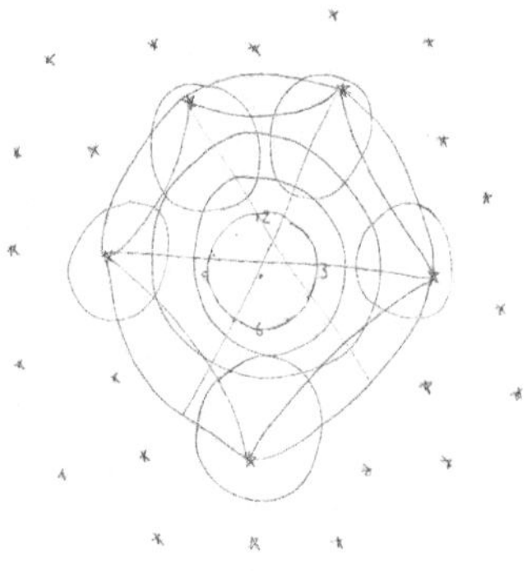

with the life force of two
my sister's energy has been passed on through me
she is very much still alive in my heart
she is moving my hands as i type
i know energy can never die
my experiences have taught me so
i know what i've seen
i know what i've felt
and no one can take that away from me

my heart beats as one
so strong
for the both of us

i'm living for two

you shall see

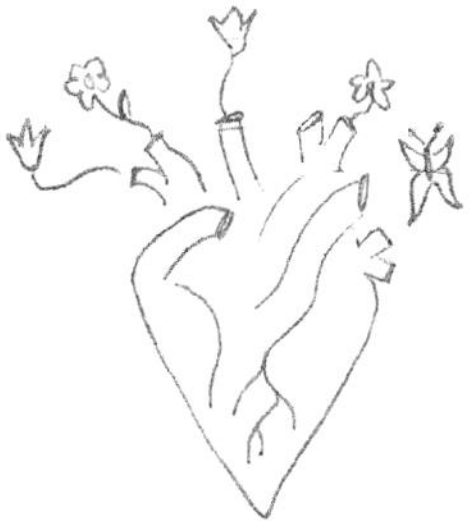

so i put the telly on
and ignore my art
but see ignoring my art
is ignoring my own heart

this resistance to myself has gotta stop.

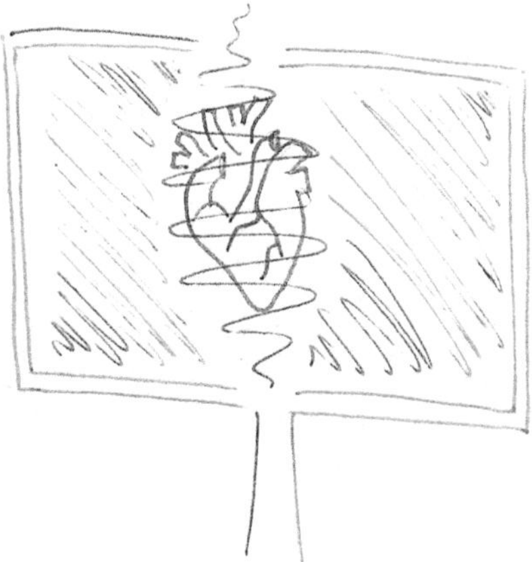

the softest hearts bear the thickest skin.

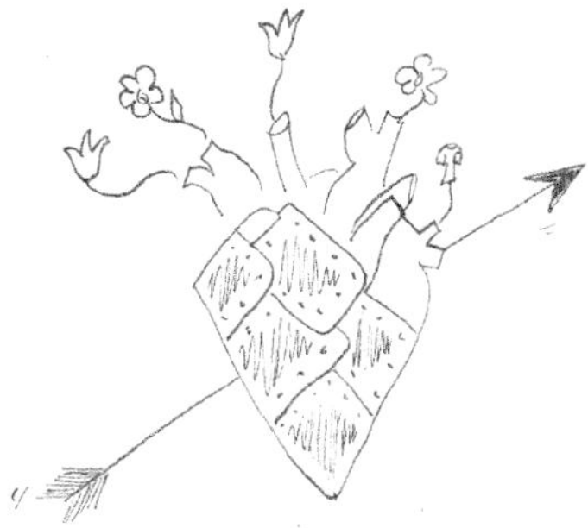

hastily playing catch up on the rest of my life
i'd cut down the years if you gave me a knife

now i write to fight and battle against time
to pass on from my soul
wisdom learnt
find in rhyme

heavens an echo away
a thin fragile line
in the middle's where i lay

i must act on the heavenly sign
to stride in my purpose
to always
and forever
praise and honour
the sacred divine

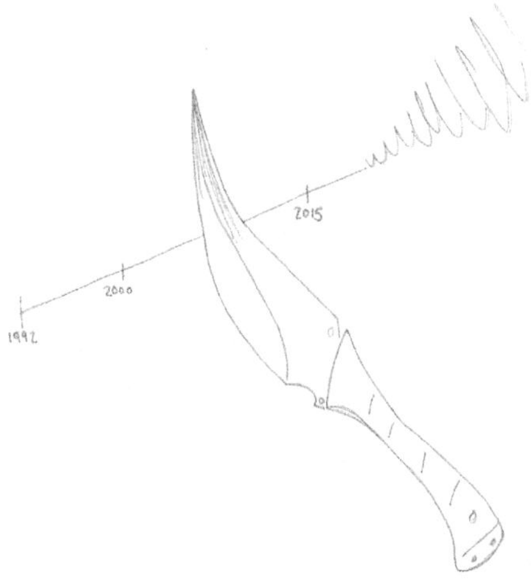

Growing pains.

i get so mad and frustrated
when i know my own potential
i know what holds me back
i know my own toxicity
i know my own anxiety
i know where it comes from
self awareness has taught me that
past traumas
so hyper aware of them
they annoy me so much
the damage they still present in my life
affecting my decisions and behaviours
patterns so hard to crack

- *give yourself time to transition my dear*
  you are aware
  integration will come
  do not give into the fear

i pray to be free one day
from the shackles of my brain
so much work inside of me i've done
to keep me calm and sane

i hope my future self is free
i hope i made you proud
for to battle one's own mind unseen
takes courage
but speaks so loud

see it takes going against the crowd
to dive deep into your wounds
but to live in chains
with no remains

- not an option

so i'll water my heart
and cherish
all the magnificent ways
she blooms

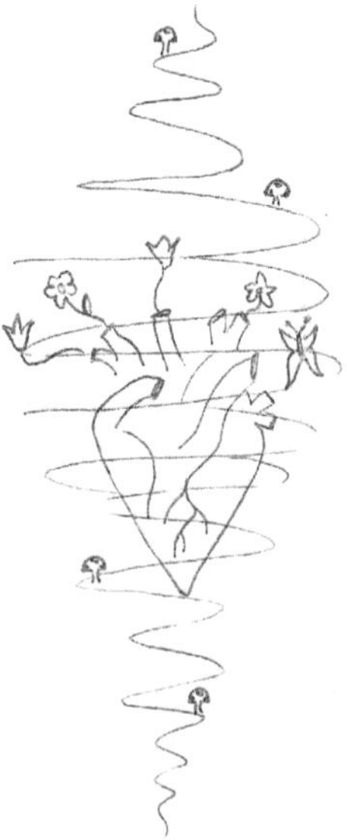

see that's the thing about fear
when we befriend it
it becomes an illusion
often times
the most beautiful awakening blossoms
from staring fear straight in the eye
and realising
it was never really fear in the first place
just a misplaced emotion
a misplaced sigh
the same chemical reaction as excitement
one that'll have you spinning high

easy mistake to make
but what a relief

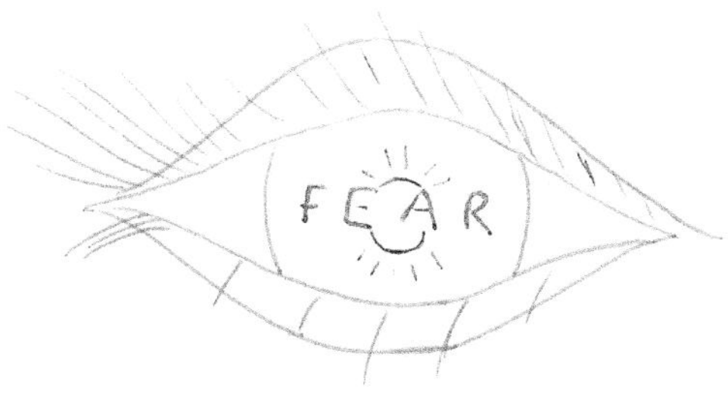

Every level has a new devil

i never told you some days i barely made it out of bed
flattened, consumed by anxious thoughts in my head

we all got light and dark within
not all will accept both sides
but it's an exhausting task
when its the dark your constantly trying to hide

-accept duality.

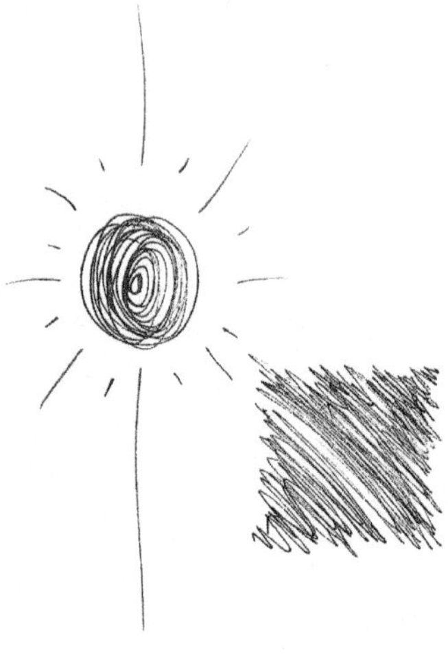

A plague

our emotions
if only we face

a pandemic engulfing the whole human race
a disease of the heart, soul and mind not in sync

unresolved

survival

will hang on the brink

- try a little tenderness

yesterday felt heavy
today's a little lighter
tomorrow's not in vain
coz her mumma raised a fighter

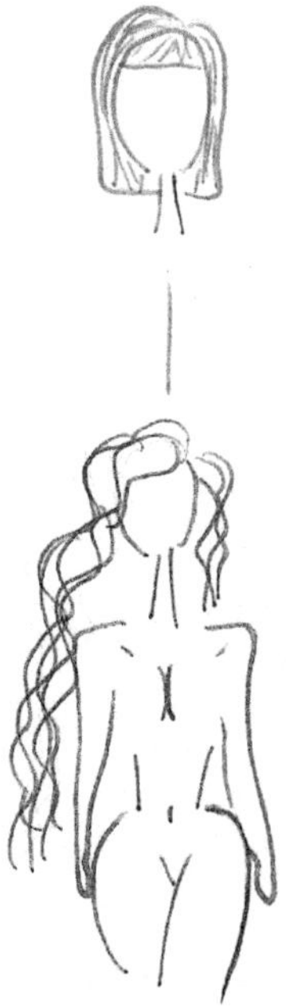

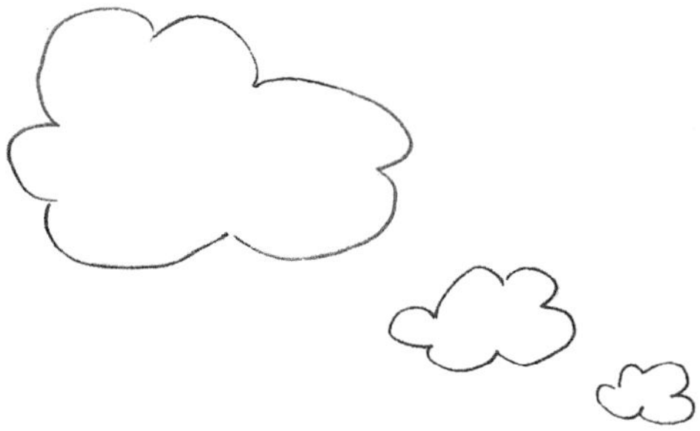

to drift again into the night
and play among the clouds
from worlds above to worlds below
childlike thoughts arouse

strange,

nothing's ever as it seems
when your vividly
more profoundly alive

in the sweet ebb and flow
and whole - e- ness
holiness

of your dreams

Dear Muse

The relief of your absence is bliss in my bones
i can breathe
i have birthed your work
in many shades and tones

Today

i am done
please lay me to rest
i hope you can see
i have given my best

tomorrow's a bright fresh new day
tomorrow
you have permission
to meet me where i lay

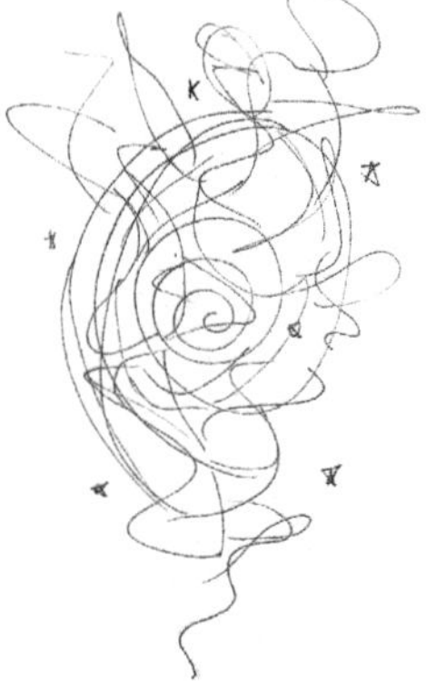

i feel more in my body today
the creative surge took me high
funny when your out of it
and reflect on the feeling
seems otherworldly
in other realms
where my restless soul could fly
looking back…

i was weightless matter
soaring the heavenly
clear blue sky

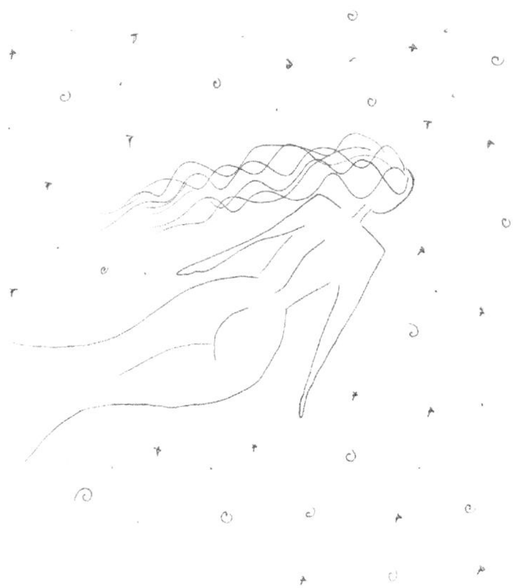

i hope i got enough out of you today

Today.

as the illusion
peels away
i see more and more of myself
ashamed of all the ways i have been living
yet there always seems to be
more empathy
at the core

shadow work

the gift that keeps giving

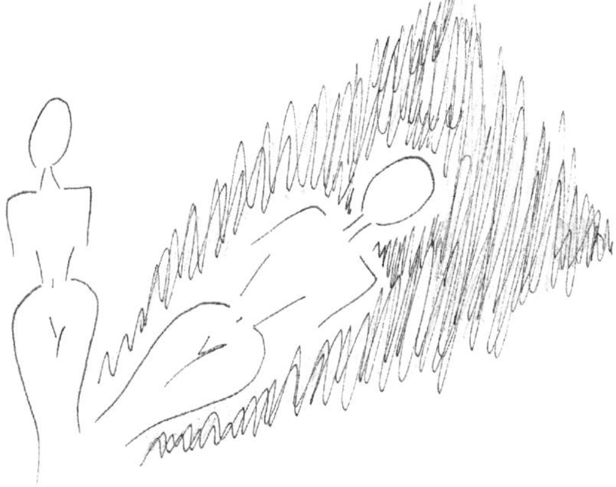

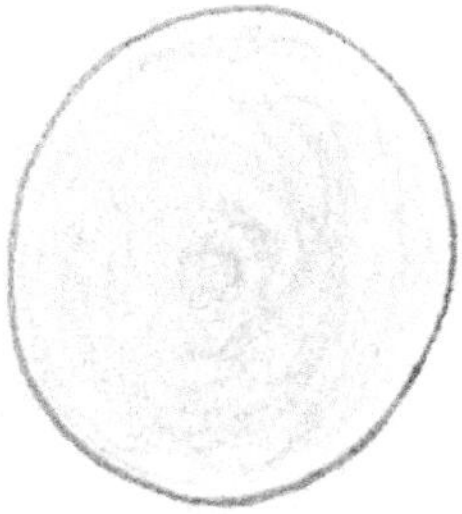

i envy those who wake with the morning sun
fresh as a daisy they bloom
for i merge with my dreams
in deep slumber it seems

i've always been more in love with the moon

a rainbow of colours her voice does project
a sentence reflecting her soul

her mind and body a deep vessel
for God's holy work
to honour his song makes her whole

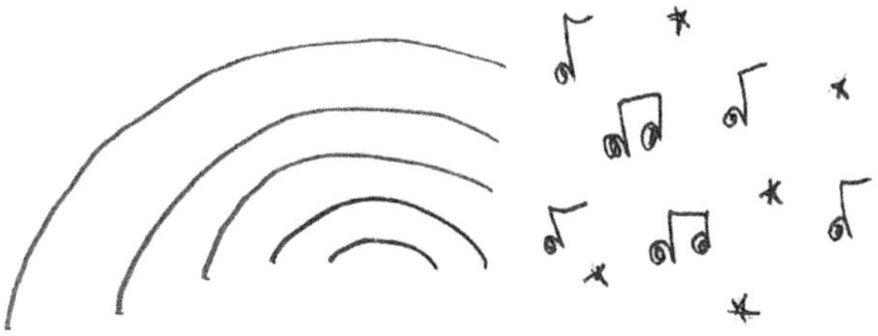

the parts of my heart not many get to see
so many parts still remain
untouched
treasured mystery

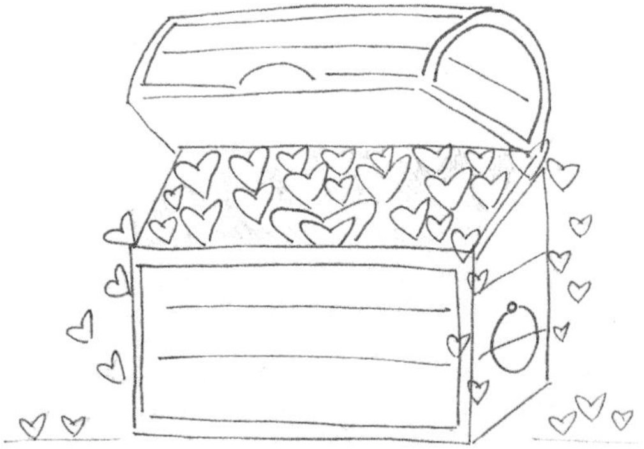

art is a mirror of humanity

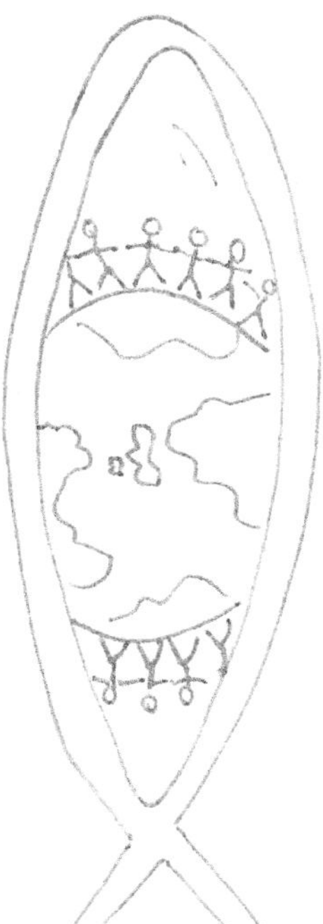

caught between different moods
different versions of me
learning that they can all coexist simultaneously
and all serve a purpose

there's a lot a lot of love

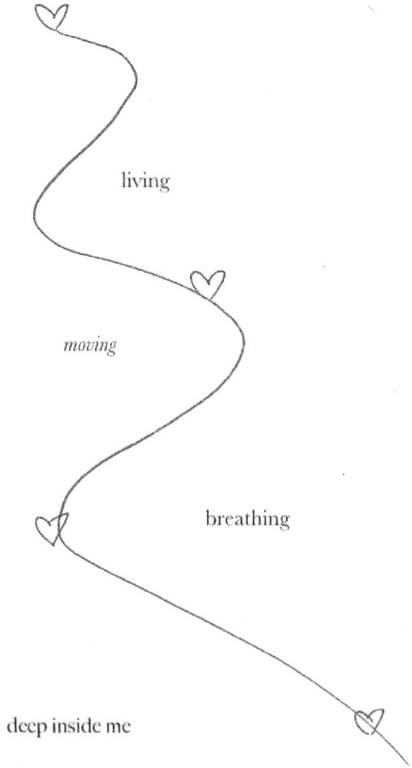

the balance between finding periods of solitude to hear my heart's intelligence, letting spirit flow through me

and being in and of this world

interacting
connecting with other humans
experiencing life as the social creatures we are

- a paradox dilemma i still find challenging at times

- i must work on the latter

Balance.

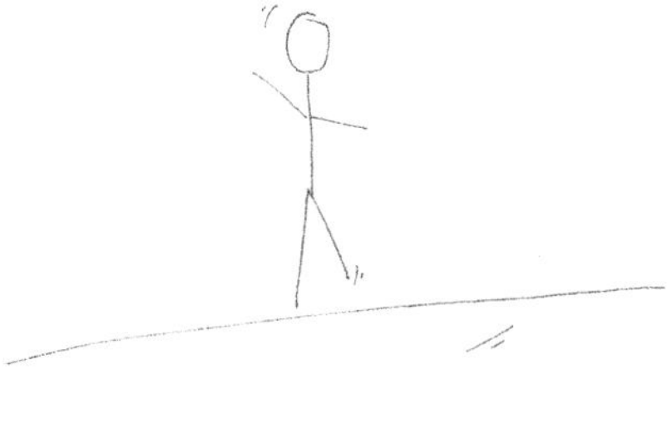

social media is a funny thing
from a heart that has so much to share and say
i wonder will anybody hear?
do i speak through the screen?
is my voice even heard?
am i ever truly really seen?
after all the purpose of life is to serve
and share what our souls here have learnt
that's how we teach each other and pass on our knowledge

but there seems to be a blockage in the ethers
maybe i'm not in the right situation or place in my life
or maybe there's just so much out there
the ethers are overloaded
yes that could be it
i've accepted this
what matters most is that you still act
share your wisdom
through the screen or not
how do you want to be remembered?
what tangible pieces of yourself do you want to leave
behind?
because we could all be gone tomorrow

this is my why
on earth as it is in Heaven
i strive everyday
to bring forth loves glory
for love is me
and i am love

and in love i am heard

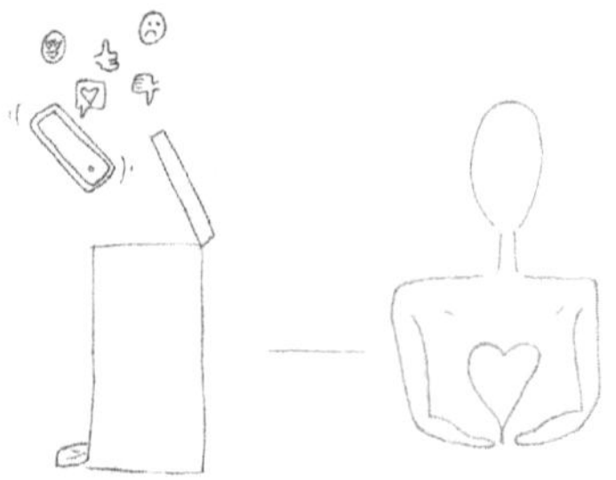

the realisation that it was the battles within my own mind
that prevented so much from happening
held me back and kept me small
blocked me from my highest self

. . .

accountability

a hard pill to swallow.

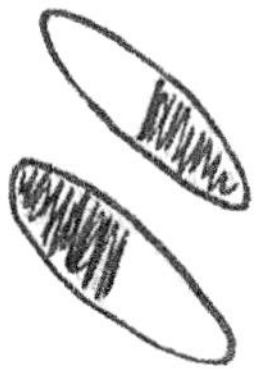

let it go
to free your soul

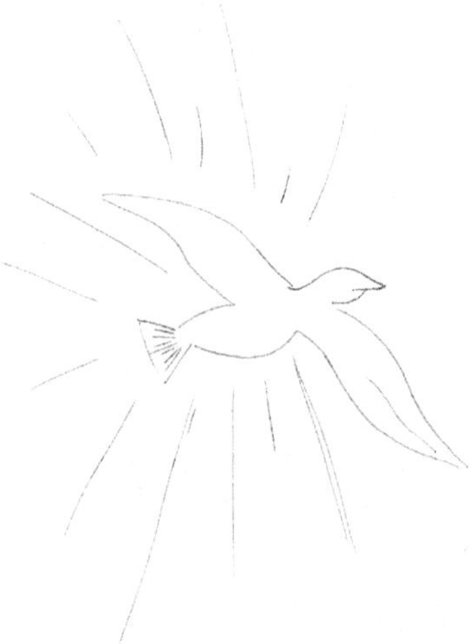

poetic heart
let down your guard
unveil the beauty
of tender scars

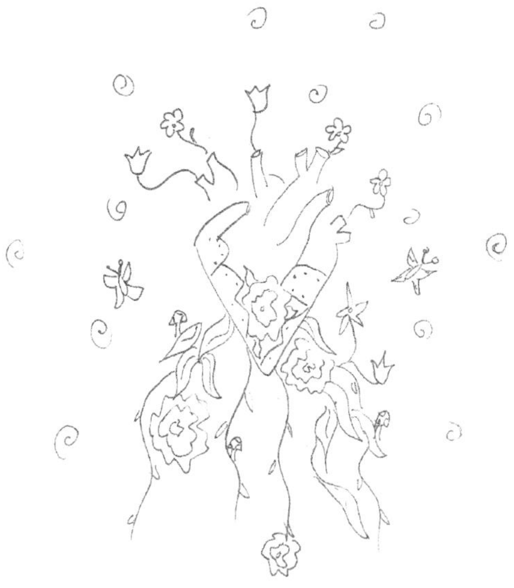

knowledge is power
teach me how to grow
fill me up to the brim with all i can know

for i'm tired of feeling i have nothing to say
when i don't know enough on the subject at play
at bay is where my voice lies hidden within
to speak of the truth shouldn't be such a sin

teach me of the world for i am her and she is me
show me all the good so i can help others see

i will learn of the ugly too

'no light without darkness'

this i know to be true

see there's a voice deep inside that is yearning to speak
and i'll be damned if that voice remains hindered and weak

so i give my prayer's over
to the powers that be
teach me knowledge of life
so i may pass you through me
i'll transform all i've learnt
and share it with thee
teach me how to

Speak
Speak

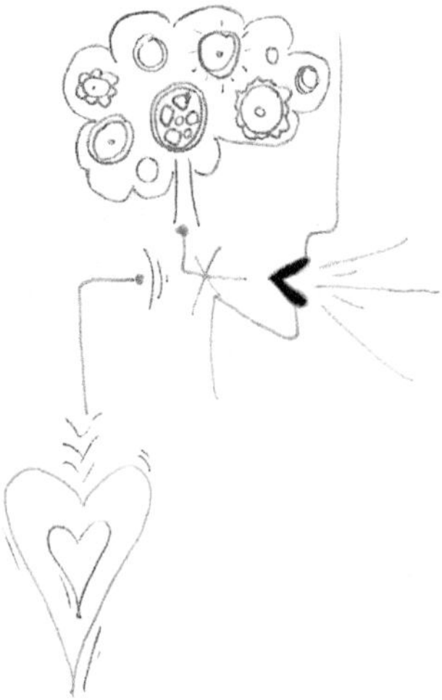

i felt like i was floating today
my mind content and spacey
as i drifted through hours in a lucid trance
a pleasant feeling
no worries to dance with
i flowed through the day like water

i think this is it

i think this is what it's like to feel better
to have a healthy mind, body and soul
for them all to unite and be working as whole

at last

i must treasure this feeling
i must bottle it and remember its
recipe
for i feel at one with the cosmos
n' something tells me
this is how it should be

everyday

it's just our silly mind that get in the
way

more play

should encourage this feeling to stay

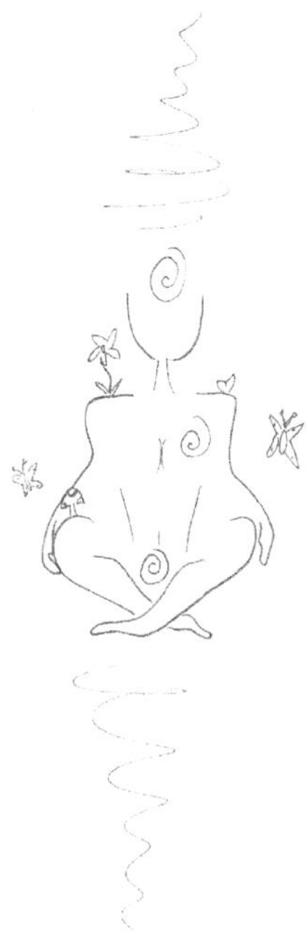

thinking back to days
where my mind would race
i couldn't get no respite from my anxious ways

as time passes
i've learnt to console myself
nothing else matters if you ain't got your health

so now i'm singing…

'rest dear one
calm your breathe
settle now
you've done your best

tomorrow will come
a brand new day
to venture new worlds
through mind's eye you'll play

and you'll play
every day

just keep playing
every day'

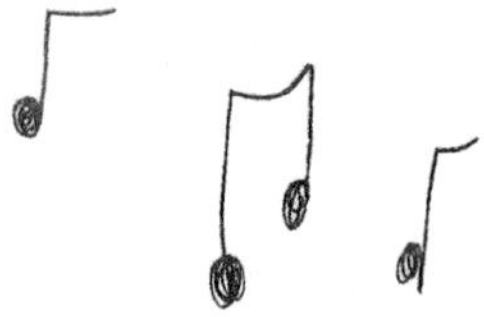

OCEAN THOUGHTS…

Ocean Thoughts 1

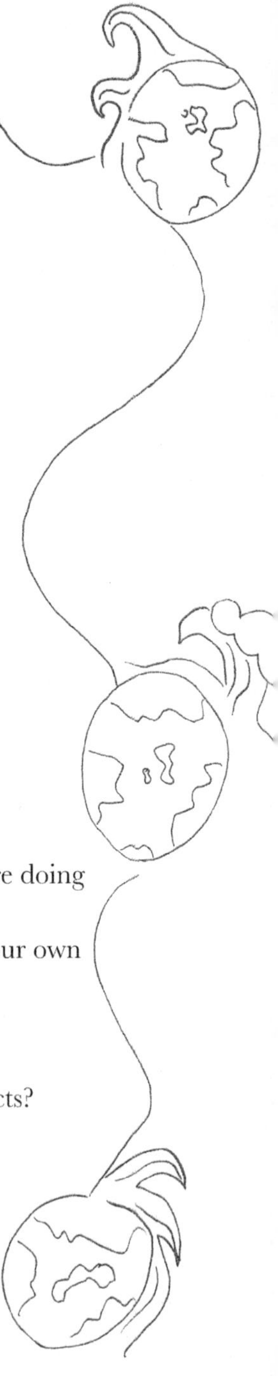

my heart cried today
as the sadness sunk into my bones

No Ocean wildlife - No humans.

if one can't survive without the other
and the ocean is an extension of us
and we are an extension of the ocean
then we're made of the same stuff
just different atoms
rearranged and reformed
would it be fair to say then
that the ocean is like another organ
that our body can't survive without?

with this concept in mind
we as a human race,
amongst many other destructive things we are doing
to damage this beautiful earth
are slowly eating and damaging our way to our own
extinction
subconsciously for the most part
i find this deeply disturbing
it goes completely against our survival instincts?

may God forgive our ignorance
and hastily wake us up…

we have to take responsibility for our actions
by killing the ocean we are killing humanity

this HAS to stop.

my heart is heavy and full of rage
it seems man's ego has outgrown itself to the point of no return
the ego has its place to help us form some sort of identity
and keep us safe in this world, sure
but i fear we have let it take over
so much disconnect to our spirit
and basic human intelligence

we have forgotten who we are…

WE ARE ALL CONNECTED
WE DESTROY MOTHER EARTH
WE DESTROY OUR EXISTENCE
WE LOOK AFTER OUR EARTH
WE LOOK AFTER OURSELVES
AND FUTURE GENERATIONS TO COME

there is not one without the other
so why are we destroying our home?!
if earth is our spaceship to orbit around the sun
we are killing our crucial crew members
- ocean life
at rapid speed

we do not own the sea
we never have done
it's this false ideology that we 'own' this planet that has got
us into this mess in the first place
sea creatures must be protected
as a crucial member of this spacecraft we call earth
without them
the human species die
simple as that

the earth will carry on orbiting the sun year after year
but the human race will be a long dead species

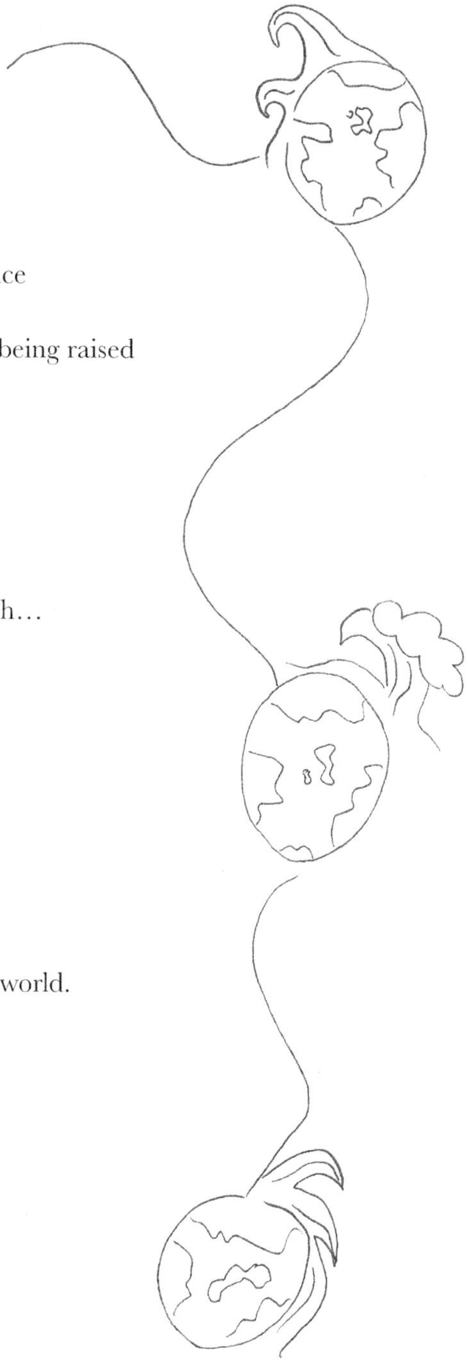

we must
dig deeper into our intelligence

i am grateful for these issues being raised
and exposed in my lifetime
it sparks some hope
however small
that if we accept our actions
and take full responsibility
for our future as humans
and for the whole planet earth…

for we are her
and she is us

we CAN help heal the planet
and breathe life into a better world.

i've heard it say
that the Creator holds the world in complete balance

light/dark
good/bad
happy/sad
rich/poor
life/death
love/hate
50/50

I don't doubt this equation
I don't doubt this pendulum
I don't doubt these scales
I could never doubt creation

but it's hard to comprehend it's confidence from down here
it feels more like humans are tipping the scales of survival
to a drastic level
consciously too
could we ever be in perfect balance?

what would happen to the universe
because from far down here it feels like a war zone
it feels like the latter side of the 50
everywhere
am i supposed to trust that it's all under control
part of a greater plan?...

or is there more you ask of yourself through us
great Creator?
i won't tamper with your scales if it's perfectly in balance
but i guess my tampering would only be you tampering
through me right?
if that's what you desire
so tamper with me in any way you see fit
let me help keep your scales in perfect balance
if it must be
but i will only play on the left side of the 50%
you know that because you are me
i am an expression of you
use me as a vessel to pour your love through
and save our essential
endangered beautiful
beloved crew

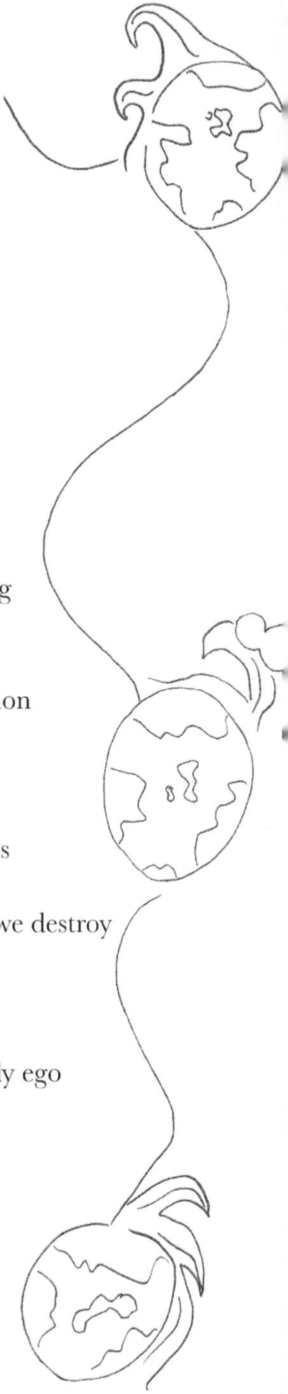

Ocean Thoughts II

the bad has got me fired up
my restless soul wont ease
when i talk of the bad
i speak of the heartbreaking destruction
mankind is causing earth

how can we destroy something so vital
to one's own existence
the existence we so obviously share
this threat on our oceans is deeply disturbing
and a huge threat to the human race
why do we turn such a blind eye?
so disappointing to see such a large proportion
of the human race
still stuck in an ignorant slumber
we are smarter than this!
our origin of intelligence is smarter than this

we are a branch of the greater intelligence we destroy
the intelligence that keeps us alive
churning our roots from the ground up
slaying our capillaries one vessel at a time
all to grow our consumption of man's greedy ego
no wonder we are all so disconnected…

on behalf of the whole human race

Mother Nature
Mamma Gia
Universe
Creator
God …

I deeply apologise
for we know not what we do
but it's about damn well time we did.

Clarity...

is one thing i have gained
so many new truths, too many to name

time in solitude is time well spent for a mind like mine
a necessity in fact
that once felt like a crime
ridiculed as boring for not complying to play
when alone time is needed to keep anxiety at bay…

a sensitive being
my intuition cuts life a knife
a double edged sword that comes with a hefty price
radar intuition
she guides me through
a blessing and a curse
when you feel pains of the world so deeply too

i absorb people's energy if i'm not careful
and that can disrupt me for days
leaving me weak at the core
and my mind in a maze

there seems to be no boundaries between my nervous
system and the outer world
my reactive response to mother nature casts my body into
a twirl
into a whirlwind of emotions that can bring me to my
knees
and just as quickly make me feel as alive as the trees
and the bees of this world
brothers and sisters of our land…

fish, mammals, birds and more
all need a helping hand
to share this ecosystem, and cohabit with them all
really does stir the urgency of the call
to save our dear planet from going extinct
Mother Earth can't survive and humanity's on the brink
we should be uniting together
with the power of our brains
this planet is under if we don't implement drastic change

my heart feels heavy knowing we've succumbed to the
reigns of man's ego

here's where my clarity runs out of ink.

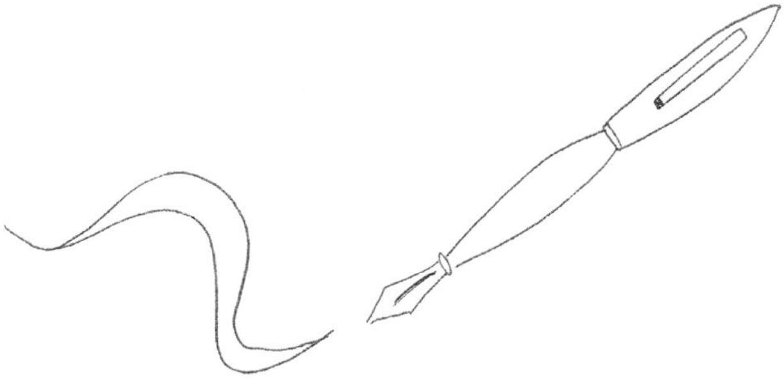

BLOOM.

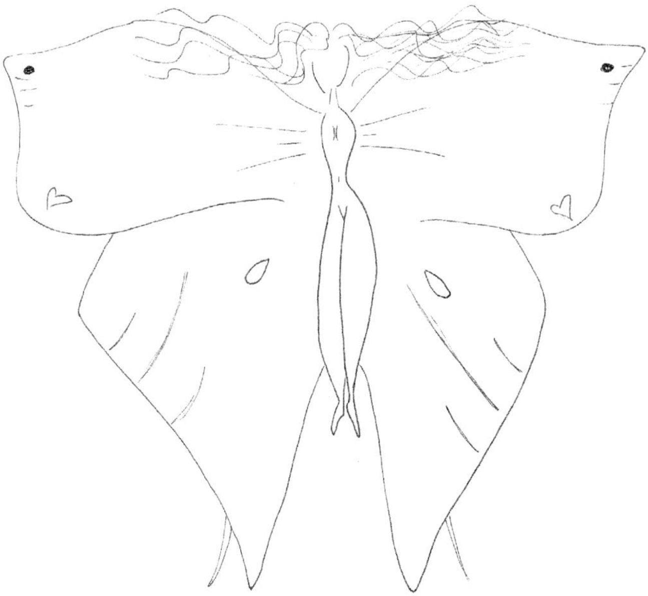

i'm excited for this next chapter of life
i feel wiser
older
more sure of myself
much more in control of my own mental health
at last
i had a lot of baggage to unpack
now i truly feel free from the pain
from this beautiful life
so much wisdom to gain

when you search deep within
you come to realise
to look elsewhere for your worth is the ultimate sin
for you will not find it in other people places or things

look inside one's heart
discover your own art
fly and let your soul freely soar

to love oneself is essential
to unlock your truest potential
n' find the courage to fearlessly roar

golden key in hand
soul purpose already planned
no hesitation step through a new door

time to discover
the sweet nectar bliss
of the infinite mystery…

More

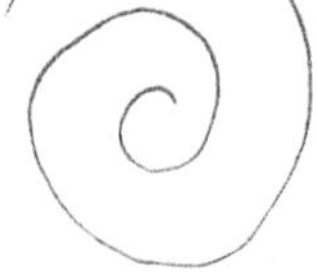

i'd hoped my future self would see
the reward was worth the pain
i promised you through thick and thin
in suffering lies wisdom to gain

haven't even scratched the surface
with what God's put on my heart

steady as we go
let's make this life a work of art

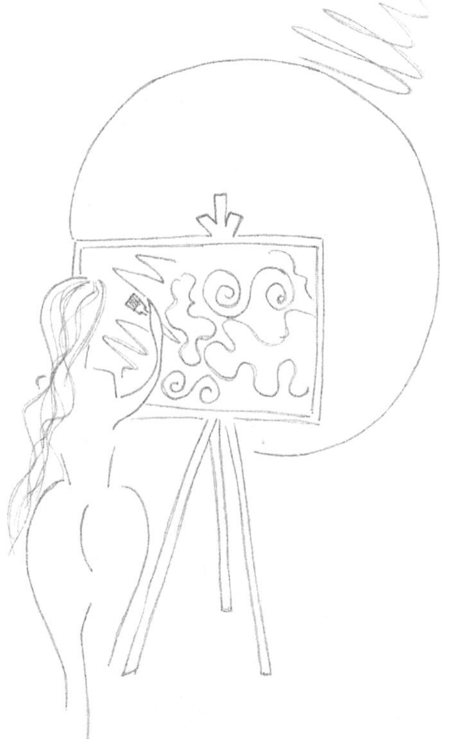

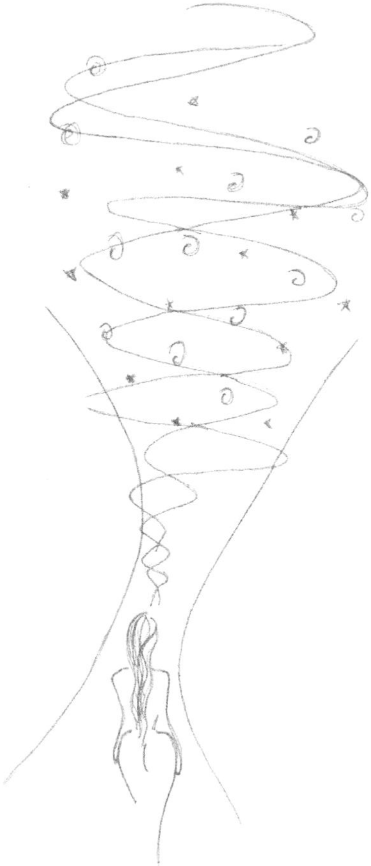

i give my trust over
to higher powers that be

to guide me into sweet
untouched treasured mystery

turn your pain into art
and your art will heal your pain

♡x

you'll realise your suffering
was never in vain.

♡x

- LJB

the art we can dig from the depths of our soul
for humanity to thrive and unite us as whole
bring forth from subconscious
now the one and only goal

in the shadows of hearts lies gold

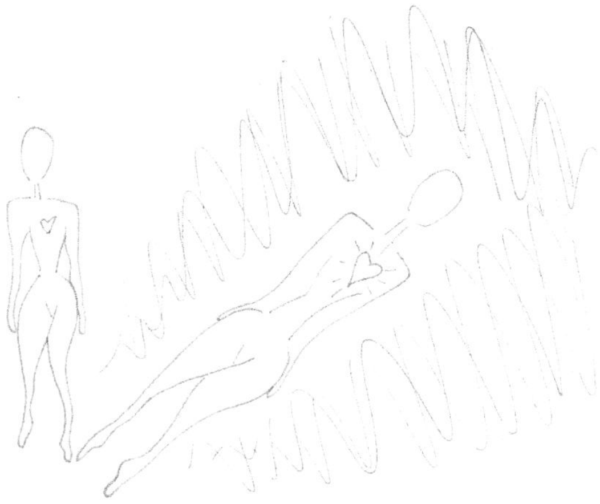

A short prayer

to the creator above
i promise to keep faith
please lead me with love

for i am you and you are me

as above

----

so below

Omnipresent

love is working through me
as love is working through you

Vessels

i am an expression of love
as you are an expression of love

all around, everything, everywhere

expressions expressing

L*OVE*

to have a relationship with the divine
is to have a relationship with your own heart
and honour its deepest desires

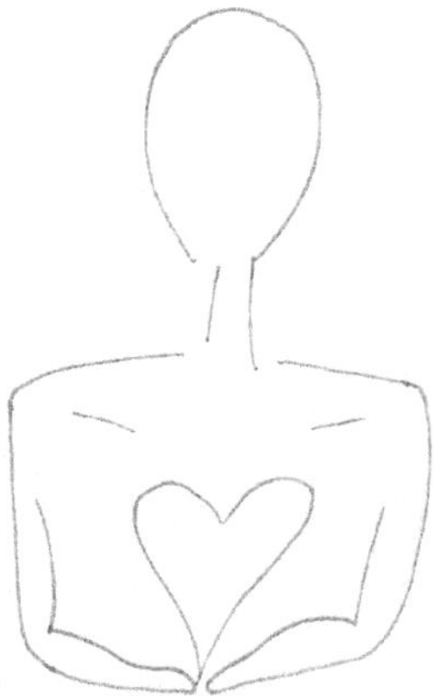

God and I met in sweet solitude …

I found…

a love that surpasses all time and space
a love far greater than the whole human race

run from vulnerability
but i can run no more

it was necessary to dig
to the depths of my core

to peel back the layers
and uncover hidden treasures
buried under false conditioning
where sweet hope sleeps whispering

join me…

free yourself from the matrix
so much more to life you'll find
you'll realise your heart is one of a kind
with a sprinkle of trust
let soul guide your mind
surrender to eternity's bliss
where tender love will hold you
true connection won't scold
you
let it mould you

- eternity's kiss

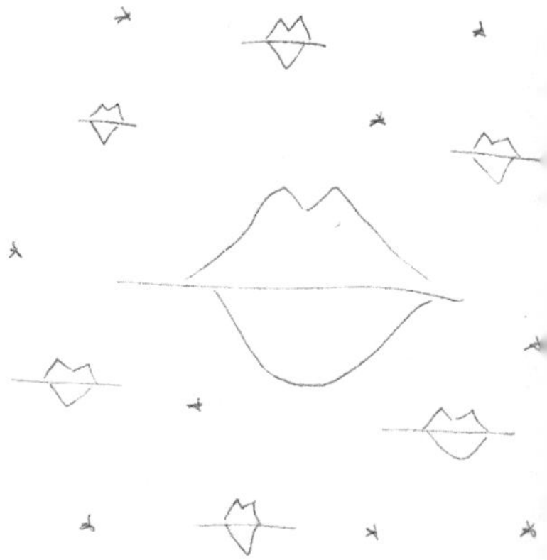

forgive me for not hearing a word you just said
i was too busy wrestling my intuition to bed
for i heard from your soul words unspoken you see
it's a blessing and a curse that's been gifted to me

your body cried in language that words cannot speak
your mind seems fragile and your soul … she is weak
right now,
there is pain
that has dimmed all your light
love's a sunken ship
hope's all out of sight

your eyes do not lie
you can no longer hide from me
i am a resting place for your embrace
no threat i bring to thee

if only you could see

me

for who i am under the disguise of my flesh
my only hope is for you and your soul to find rest

see i was too busy hearing words you're body left unspoke
you seem intimidated and nervous by the thoughts
i provoke

let go

I am safe

her spirit is exquisitely, intriguingly
old and wise
her heart is youthful and young

her mind…
it can wonder from time to time
but when synced

see her shine like the sun

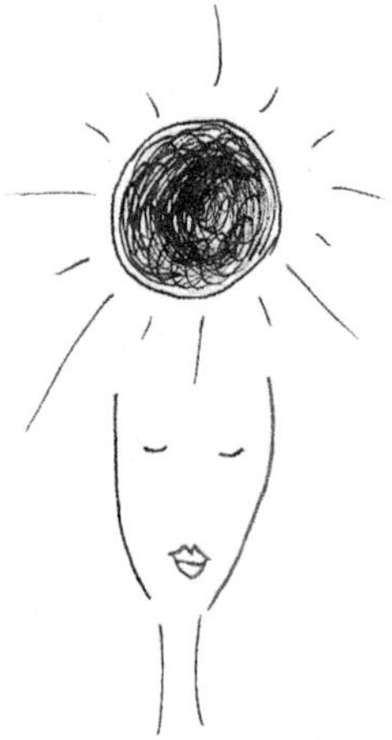

most powerful when hidden
shines brightest in the dark

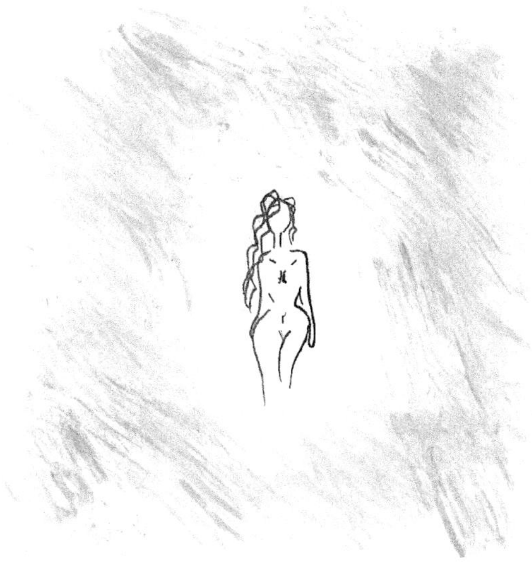

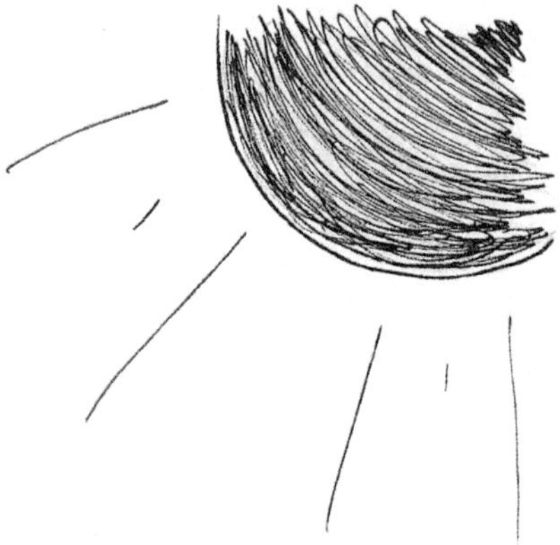

it's more sunny than rainy in my mind these days

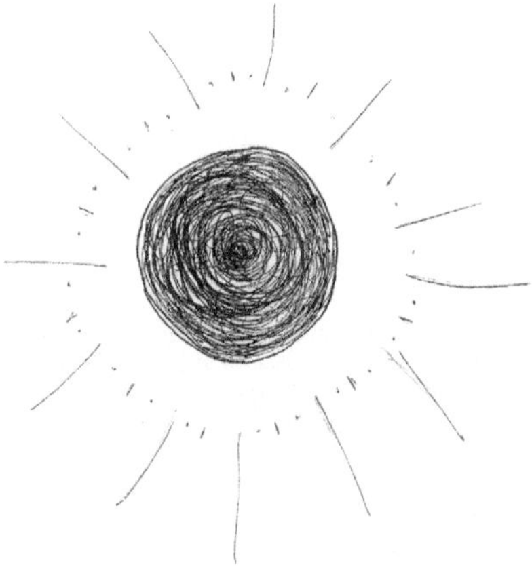

strange how lucid my mind seems
moments pass by and evolve so quickly
hastily moving from one moment to the next
incredible when you master the art
of slowing down time with your breath
to become more aware of space
the minutes between the hours
the seconds within the minutes
these moments of pure clarity and presence
oneness with the world

peace

so much power in this space
power to feel more than your human
power to drift beyond your own realm of consciousness
power to adjust your perspective and see past the illusion
past the veil to heavens gates
where time is nothing more than a concept
where time is not linear

suspended in *weightless* love

Heaven

Heart to Heart

underwater is where i hear you the loudest
see you in my mind's eye the clearest
the water surrounding my ears
makes an internal echo chamber
it blocks off all noise and muffles the outside world
just enough so i can hear your rhythm
steady as the beating drum
the pounding of my heart booms through my ribcage
sending ripples of frequencies that engulfs my senses
i bow to your greatness
the exquisite mechanism that you are
you fuel my engine
my body
i have so much to thank you for
you beat at just the right pace to carry me in this world
i'm astounded by your presence of beauty and grace
i honour your immense strength and power
your resilience inspires me so
i marvel at your courage to keep pulsing
after all you have been through
it's hard to believe i ever thought external validation
and approval
was all i needed in this world to feel whole
i was so disconnected from the magnificence of my own
vessel
when the pain was too much and heartache reduced me
to tears
you kept beating
i feel ashamed for how i neglected and mistreated you so

Forgive me…

i needn't have looked no further than my own heart
for courage
when i was drowning in the depths of my shadows
you have this beautiful way of repairing yourself
living again to see another sun
another moon
your intuitive skills are impeccable
it's you i seek guidance and take direction from
i listen for your instructions for what to do next
you are my compass
my home port
may i never forget
sometimes your innate intelligence overwhelms my brain
it can have a hard time interpreting and processing your
feeling codes at first
but she gets there in the end
i will do everything in my power to keep you strong
and healthy
i look forward to all the lessons you have yet to teach me
all the beautiful memories we are yet to share
the outside world can be so daunting, so distracting
so underwater
in tranquillity
i pray
i always meet you there

My Strong Sturdy Tender Heart

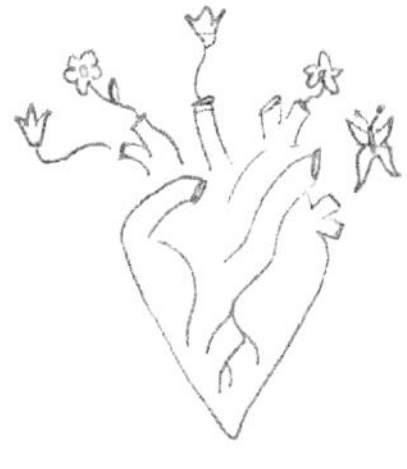

my soul is honoured to embody this vessel

Thank you

Mamma Gaia

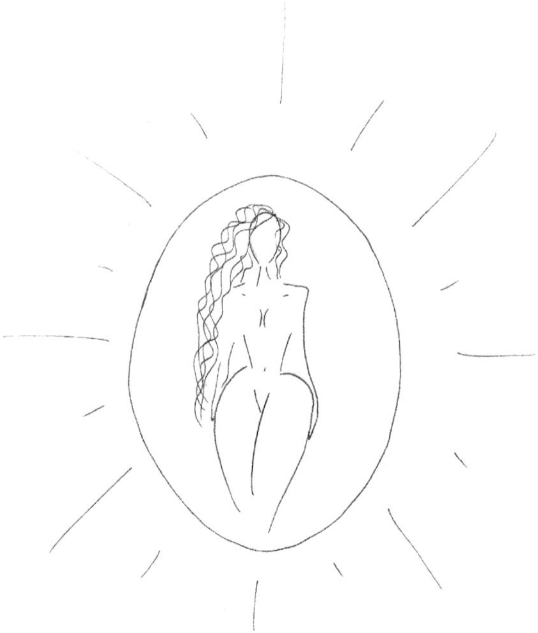

the innocence of children
so pure
unstained
free to live and revel in the playground of their
imagination
no pain
free to discover themselves
to express themselves fully
laugh when they find things funny
cry when they're upset
their shift between emotions
seamless
then in a blink of an eye
they forget

no concept of time
no stress
we must not let our child within us die
as we grow older we evolve
into different versions of ourselves
but our inner child stands firm
she is our building block from which we grow
and discover other aspects of ourselves and learn

honour her
for she will always
guide us back home
to our childlike nature within

Masks.

we all wear masks at times
to hide aspects of our souls
multiple masks for different modes
driving
teaching
singing
writing
dancing
cooking
cleaning
parenting
and the rest

the ego wears the most deceiving mask of all
Commedia dell'arte
the ego serves to protect us
a mask to protect our identity
worn like a prison cage around our heart
fiercely protecting it from the pains and hurts of this world
to hide behind a mask…
a necessity at times to get through life
different masks to endure us through trouble and strife
the outer protective shell of me
hiding the depths of my soul not many get to see

our flesh an outer mask too
for how someone looks on the outside can be
so very different
and bare no resemblance to their inner world
their soul
we can adjust and adapt to so many different environments

a trait that unites us all
so many different versions of ourselves we can experience
and explore
shedding skin like a snake slithering through a new door
each chapter a new season welcomed
many a mask has been worn at some point or another
self preservation of one's own soul
scared to show people the vulnerabilities of our hearts
never accepting ourselves as whole
but why?
it’s so damaging
to not speak from the heart
it’s truly a poison to the soul
i cannot bear it
why does society not speak from the heart
like we did in our youth?
when the heart is our guiding light
the compass to our truth
we’ve grown so disconnected to our internal rhythm
we’ve had no choice but to wear a mask
anyone will do
other peoples too
exploring different fits
one after the next
never truly comfortable with any of them
but they hide and avoid that voice from inside
that is yearning to speak
we dare not listen
rather remain a phoney and weak
for to listen would cause too much upheaval
too much introspection of the self
could cause confliction and reveal our evil…

the reputation we have built for ourselves
exposed if we remove our mask

after every mask i've tried and worn
multiple masks have left me torn
between different identities
and different versions of myself
one here, one there to accumulate more wealth
but my health was suffering underneath it all
my masks of protection began to crumble and fall
i could not function without the strength of my shield
the flesh i wore had not changed
so the cracks did not show
how could they not see?
that i was longing to stop
pause and heal
little did i know, nature was stripping me away
pulling me down deep to the chambers of my heart
to face shadows i had never met before
if our bodies and minds were transparent
if our hearts were transparent
honesty would lead the way
the intuitive
emotionally intelligent
see through the facade
and read our hearts clear as day

so you see my love
wear a mask if you must
but do not think you're fooling anyone
for the awakened eye can see right through
not matter how sturdy the ego
get back to heart's love
and trust
it's the right thing to do

authenticity will lead you to you.

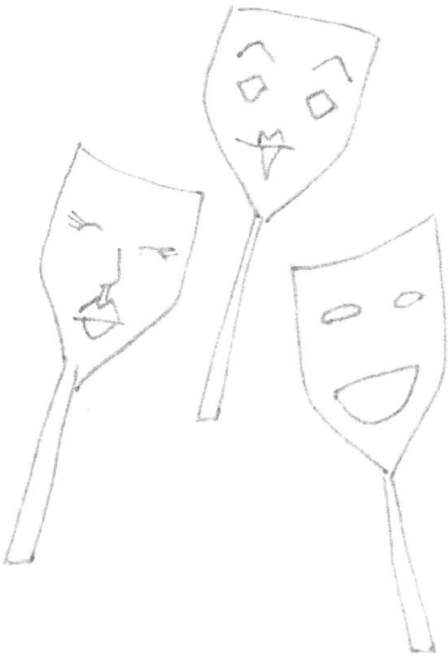

I close my eyes

Cornwall 29.04.2021 - mollies 6th year anniversary

i hear the soothing rumble of the waves caressing the shore
i splay my hands and feel the tiny soft grains of sand
escaping through the sieve of my palms
i see white hazy lights dance behind my eyelids
as the sun makes her home upon my face
i feel of my body, but not it in
as if i'm a visitor hovering over myself
admiring the beauty of my surroundings
i so deeply feel apart of
my mind wonders through all time and space
there is nothing that separates the air that dances around my skin
from my skin itself
my soul feels light
weightless
content
still and calm
i bask in the bliss of this moment
the next, the next, then the next
savouring every detail
i feel my heart beat pulse in my chest
a steady rhythmic tempo
a sure sign i am in this body still

the sea never gives
not even for a second
white noise in the background
she becomes the soundtrack to my day

a dog barks
adults laugh
children in the distance play

the waves move gracefully to the flow of their master
they do not question where they land
they do not hesitate to swoon and play among the sand
they do not apologise for their ripple effects
or for the unforgettable echo they so passionately project

we too can be like waves
we too can dance with life and never be afraid
we too can follow our God given spirit
for the divine commands the tides of our souls
to swim divinity's course is bliss
a call you don't wanna miss
as it's truly worth it's loving weight in gold

CREATURES OF LOVE

Octopus

the most fascinating creature
great creator you never cease to amaze me
with your spectacular creations
this one had me in awe of your almighty intelligence
the way you crafted yourself into this truly magnificent
creature
to experience yourself...
i'm in awe
malleable
the ability to mould into any texture, size, shape or colour
you change with each new environment
the chameleon of the seas
your art of deception
how you cover yourselves in shells to protect yourself
from predators
genius

you adapt with the seasons
embracing them all
hibernating in winter
collecting food in the fall
you re-grow yourself when injured from your prey
you overcome yourself and rise again
with each new waking day

your ability to see and sense safety from a human
a bond so magical and pure
it was at that moment
i saw a reflection of me in you
an intelligent love
a blissful recognition of souls to adore...

i bow in awe of you
intelligent creature
thank you for dancing with us in your existence
you helped me realise we share it all
intelligent soul
my heart hears your call

a divine connectedness
tugs at my heart
we are one
truly in awe of you

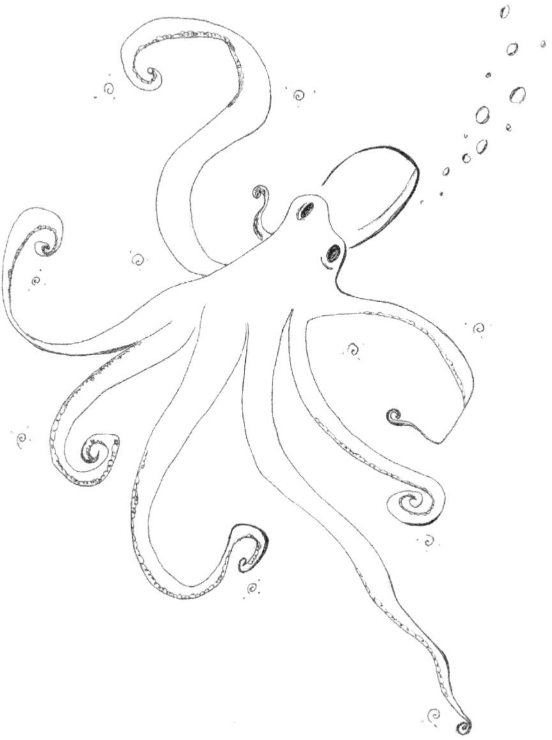

Yellow Butterfly…

you have returned to greet me in the sun
you pause all my worries and make me feel at one
how did one earn the presence of your delicate grace
your beauty pulls focus through all time and space

a sweet tender smile you lay upon my face
you never fail to catch my eye
you twirl and soar
a precious sight to adore
as your radiance beams in the sky

your bravery to fly inspires me so
from the tomb of your cocoon you so delicately grow
you give me faith in life to strive for more
to honour the intelligence that lies at our core

to transform from a creature of the ground
a metamorphosis of your soul
a sweet reckoning you found

yellow butterfly
i ponder and wonder at your existence
perhaps we're more alike than it seems
for i too have transformed and felt light in the air
when i'm dancing at one with my dreams…

yellow butterfly
i marvel at your elegance
i'm honoured to bask in your presence
yellow butterfly
i am peacefully
so dearly
humbled to reside in your essence

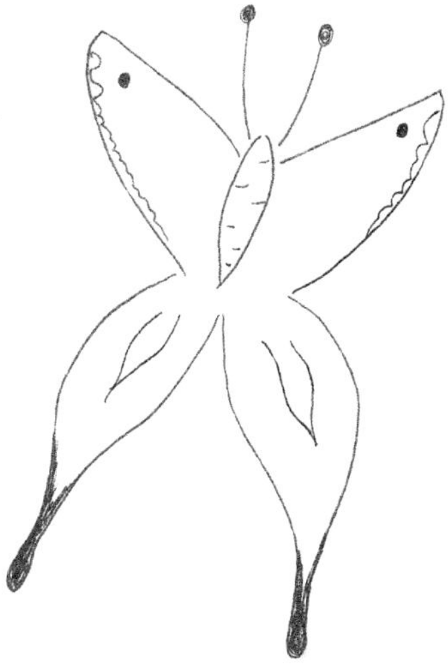

Bee

as i wake from my slumber
i hear the faint buzz of your arrival
your presence echoes through my lucid dream
with a resonance so tribal
you've come to assist me and help me rise
to a beautiful day it would seem
always on time
7.30 am on the dot
outside my window
in the exact same spot
everyday
just you
on your own

but there's no flowers here
no honey
why do you stop by?
you seem adamant my dear
no fear as you fly

i can only imagine you've found a home within these walls
a cosy respite from your day
through the tangerine brick you crawl…

well
how times have changed
for fear you used to cast
but now i delight in your presence
and great purpose at last

you pollinate flowers and breathe life to our lungs
and who better to help me rise with the sun
you entice me out of my sleep
a new fuzzy friend outside my window
my new fuzzy friend i shall keep

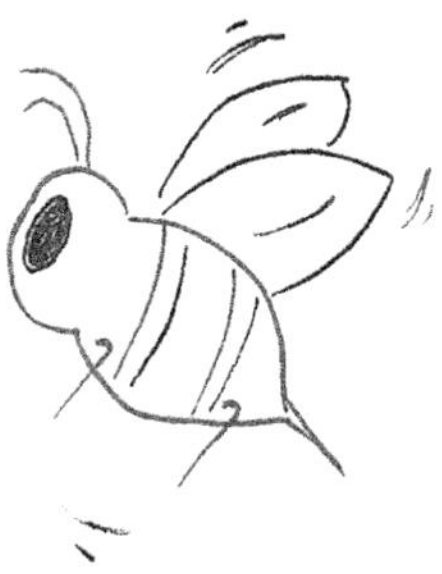

we must look to nature for hope
a divine reflection it mirrors to us
reassurance we see in our ability to evolve and transform
when we surrender and trust in the yolk
of our great creator who binds us all

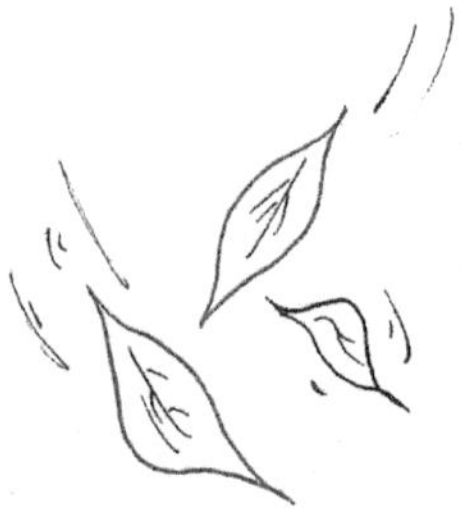

Borrowed Breath.

we are all living on borrowed breath
would you treat your neighbour differently
if you knew their time on earth was coming to an end?
aren't we all one step closer to the end of our lives
every day?

every encounter
every interaction
every exchange
every moment
is sacred time you'll never get back

we are all on loan to this Earth

appreciate the beauty in each other
appreciate the lessons in everything
we are all here to help each other grow
to experience our greatest potential
in the short time we have

time never rewinds
the great creator see's everything

it's in your best interest
to become the best version of yourself
to live up to your greatest grand design
your soul's purpose

live fully and always
and forever
be kind

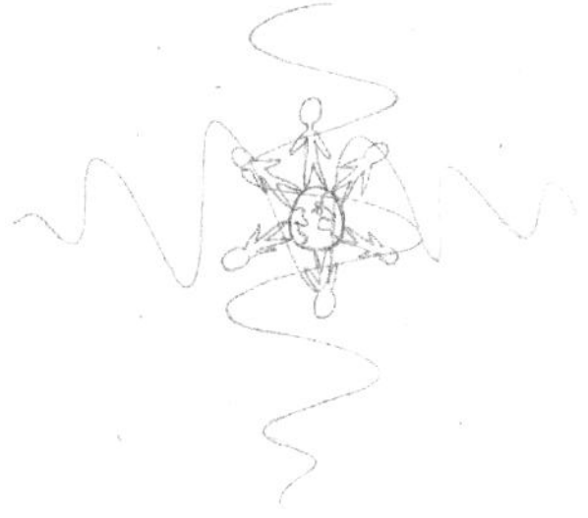

to anyone seeking or searching for answers
for the truth of this conflicting existence

Advice
if i may

maybe it's time to stop searching outward
and start looking inward

realise that you are love
love is who you are
within every cell
every atom
there is no separation
only blind spots
only that which you cannot see

so dig deep
explore yourself
every aspect of yourself
the good
the bad
and the ugly too

do not be afraid
you might just find what you're looking for

x

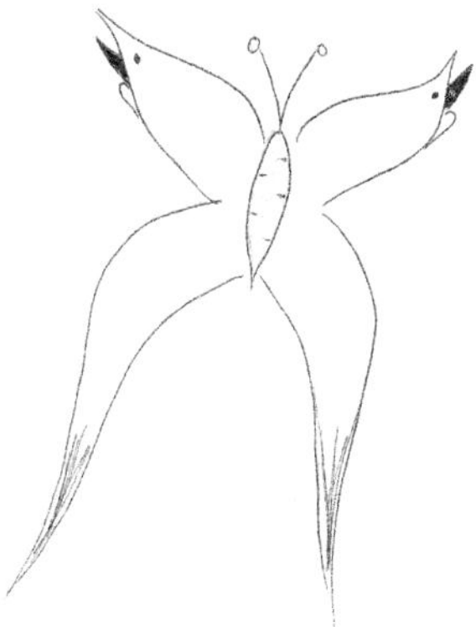

when i create something i'm proud of
i genuinely see it back as a third person
completely forgetting the process it took to create
for i know it was not solely me
i could not be capable of such things
i am merely a vessel receiving downloads
from a higher source
therefore i do not applaud myself or my ego
i stand back and give thanks and praise
to higher powers that be
that's how i know to trust the work
that's how i know what work to trust
that's when i know
i can divinely and forever
trust in me

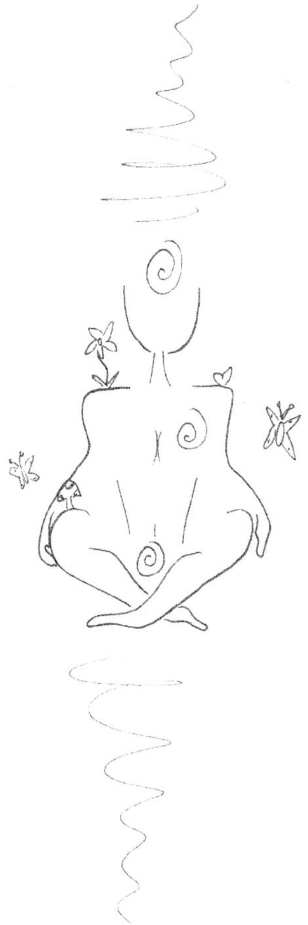

...

i get it now
why your disrespect felt so raw

you did not know of my worth
i knew not of her either
i had not grown into myself
to find her i had to crumble and claw

so many parts of me were left stale from neglect
how could i ever have possibly expected respect

well my old friend
time has made a Queen out of me
i have grown into everything i ever hoped i would be
and more
so much more
in ways truly unexpected

i have blossomed and bloomed
from my sacred holy wound
i've found love in the shadows of my flaws
i've found love at the depth of my core

now there's peace where i lay
with my troubles at bay
like a lion with courage

hear me ROARRR...

Printed in Great Britain
by Amazon

26767195R00071